POPE JOHN PAUL II
PRAYS THE LITANY
OF THE

Sacred Heart
of Jes

POPE JOHN PAUL II
PRAYS THE LITANY
OF THE
Sacred Heart of Jesus

Our Sunday Visitor Publishing Division
Our Sunday Visitor, Inc.
Huntington, Indiana 46750

With the exception of some editorial changes and the addition of the Foreword, this work is substantially the same as published in the October-December 1990 special edition of *Prayer and Service* and has been reprinted with the permission of the General Office of the Apostleship of Prayer, Borgo S. Spirito, 5 — C.P. 6139-00195, Rome, Italy.

Our Sunday Visitor Publishing Division
Our Sunday Visitor, Inc.
200 Noll Plaza
Huntington, Indiana 46750

ISBN: 0-87973-478-7
LCCCN: 91-66666

PRINTED IN THE UNITED STATES OF AMERICA

The artwork by William Cladek (copyright © 1985 by the Apostleship of Prayer, Buffalo, New York) appearing in this work has been made available through the courtesy of Msgr. Walter O. Kern of the Diocese of Buffalo.

Cover design by Rebecca J. Heaston

478

Dedicated to the memory of the Apostle of the Heart of Jesus, Saint Margaret Mary Alacoque, on the 300th anniversary of her death, October 17, 1690

TABLE OF CONTENTS

Foreword

The Litany of the Sacred Heart of Jesus unfolds in stages:

The earlier invocations focus on the communion, in eternal love, of the Heart of Christ with the Godhead, reminding us that the Spirit and Mary are the guides to this fountain of life and holiness, so rich in goodness and patience, wisdom and knowledge.

The invocations then invite us to recognize and share the treasures of the Heart of Christ.

The final invocations call to mind Christ's mission to a sinful world in loving solidarity with all who suffer the consequences of their own sins and the sins of others.

About the time that Pope John Paul II reached the halfway point in his series of Sunday Angelus messages on the invocations of the Litany of the Heart of Jesus, a ferment of devotion to Christ's Heart was rising in Brazil. It emanated from a group of priests, sisters, and brothers belonging to congregations with ties to the spirituality of the Sacred Heart of Christ. They began organizing a congress on this spirituality and its implications for pastoral activities in today's society.

The Congress was held in October 1988. Some three hundred religious representing sixty congregations attended, plus lay representatives from a dozen dioceses. The conclusions of the Congress were summed up in a message centered on communion and fidelity: communion with the Son, who reveals the Trinity's love for all; fidelity to the Church, which carries on Christ's mission to the world.

"Rooted in biblical revelation," the Congress message

says, "and lived in Christian tradition, this devotion is encouraged by the teaching Church and assimilated in faith by the people of God. . . .

"An authentic spirituality of the Heart of Jesus is a balanced spirituality. It guarantees a balance between faith and life, between contemplation and social commitment, and between the devotional practices of popular tradition and the current demands of prayer and celebration. . . .

"Those who commit themselves to live and spread the spirituality of the Heart of Jesus," the Congress concludes, "have as their mission the integral proclamation of Jesus and his message and the integral liberation of the human person, in accord with the exigencies of a just and fraternal society, the civilization of love desired by the Father and sign of the eternal kingdom."

It is with deep gratitude to Pope John Paul II that we renew our commitment to the Church's mission and this civilization of love, the Kingdom of the Heart of Christ. We ponder the Pope's insights into this mission and civilization of love as, individually and in groups, we pray the invocations of the Litany of the Heart of Jesus. Surely the Pope will consider himself well rewarded for his efforts in these Angelus messages as we transform these prayers into daily actions, at the same time bringing to our prayer the persons and situations so dear to the Heart of the Redeemer.

Rev. John Vessels, S.J.
International Secretary
General Office of the Apostleship of Prayer
Rome

Introduction

In November 1989, Pope John Paul II completed a series of Sunday Angelus messages begun in 1985, the longest series thus far devoted to a single subject. His topic: the Litany of the Sacred Heart of Jesus.

The completed series consists of thirty-three meditations on the invocations of the Litany: twelve given from June to September during the summer of 1985, and ten from June to August during the summer of 1986. The series was then interrupted for themes dealing with the Marian Year 1987-88. Reflections on the Litany were resumed with nine talks given from July to September during the summer of 1989, and the final two during November 1989.

Pope John Paul II and the Litany

Well-known is Pope John Paul's personal devotion to the Heart of Jesus, even before he was elected pope, and in fact (as he himself has said) from his boyhood onward.

As cardinal archbishop of Krakow, in a pastoral letter of June 11, 1965, on the occasion of the 200th anniversary of the establishment of the Feast of the Sacred Heart of Jesus (celebrated first of all in Poland), he refers to the Litany and quotes what seems to be his favorite invocation: "Heart of Jesus, fountain of life and holiness."

In his first encyclical letter as pope he quotes the same expression, "fountain of life and holiness," referring it to the Eucharist, but he gives as his source the Litany of the Heart of

Jesus. On other occasions he has also quoted this invocation more than any other.

Pope John Paul has frequently commented, on various occasions and under differing circumstances, on many aspects of the mystery of Christ's love under the symbolism of his Heart; and among traditional practices of the devotion, the Litany is certainly one of his favorites, which he has often recommended to others.

On June 20, 1979, during his first year as pope, in a general audience on the topic *Let us learn to read the mystery of the Heart of Jesus*, Pope John Paul had said: "The beautiful Litany to the Sacred Heart of Jesus is composed of many similar words — even more, they are exclamations of admiration for the riches of the Heart of Christ. Let us attentively meditate on them on this day" (Solemnity of the Heart of Jesus).

On June 27, 1982, the Holy Father devoted a Sunday Angelus message to a reflection on the Litany and quoted seven of its invocations. Although this is not one of the series of reflections on the individual invocations which began in 1985, it serves as a general meditation on the Litany and is included in this collection as the first of the Angelus messages on the Litany.

On July 1, 1984, in an Angelus message on the Heart of Jesus entitled *In the Heart of Christ there is a synthesis of all the mysteries of our faith*, the Pope had a few words to say about the Litany: "During the entire month of June, the Church has placed before us the mysteries of the Heart of Jesus, the God-Man. These mysteries are expressed in a penetrating way in the Litany of the Sacred Heart, which can be sung, which can be recited, but above all which ought to be meditated."

Toward the end of a homily during a Votive Mass of the Heart of Jesus, celebrated at the Airport of Vancouver, Canada, on September 19, 1984, the Holy Father quoted a number of invocations from the Litany.

Arrangement of this collection

This collection consists of thirty-four Angelus messages of Pope John Paul II on the Litany of the Heart of Jesus: thirty-three of them are meditations on individual invocations of the Litany given during 1985, 1986, and 1989. Also included is another Angelus message given before the series began on June 27, 1982, which is a meditation on the Litany.

In giving his meditations on the Litany, Pope John Paul did not always follow the order in which the invocations are arranged in the Litany itself. Nor did he always devote one talk to each invocation.

The talks vary in length. At times, when other topics also called for his attention and comment, such as the conferring of the Sacrament of Confirmation, the Pope restricted comments on the Litany that day to only a few words.

To simplify the arrangement here and to facilitate use of this collection for spiritual reading and meditation, it seemed best to arrange the talks in the order in which the invocations are found in the Litany. The date when the talk was given is indicated at the beginning of each talk. Where two invocations are discussed in one talk, the talk is given under one of them with a reference under the other.

Even with these variations in the talks themselves, the total number of talks is the same as the number of invocations, namely, thirty-three.

Since these talks of the Holy Father are meditations on the invocations of the Litany, it did not seem appropriate to add further comments or introductions to each but to let the meditations speak for themselves.

Two general characteristics of these meditations may be noted briefly. First, without making the talks an exegetical study, the Pope indicates the deeply scriptural basis of the invocations of the Litany by incorporating the biblical phrases and sources into his meditations. Second, these messages were given before the Sunday recitation of the Marian prayer of the Angelus. Consequently they have a clear reference to the mystery of the incarnation and to Mary the Mother of God, who leads us to the Heart of her Son.

How to pray the Litany today

Pope John Paul II has often recommended praying the Litany, especially each day during June, the month dedicated to the Sacred Heart of Jesus. Praying the Litany, in the Pope's own words, means reciting, singing, and above all meditating on the Litany.

We do not have processions today in the way they were once common in the past. But we can still pray the Litany individually or in groups, or even sing it as the Pope does. But probably the greatest spiritual value to be derived from these Angelus messages of the Holy Father will be to use them for meditation and contemplation.

It is clear that the Pope intends them as meditations to be used as aids to personal prayer. They are his personal reflections on the Litany, which he offers to others as a stimulus to meditate on the Heart of Jesus more fruitfully.

A final suggestion

Pope John Paul has on other occasions referred to the *Jesus prayer*, a form of prayer traditionally practiced in Eastern spirituality, especially Russian, which emphasizes what we know but tend at times to overlook: prayer must come from the heart. Hence the *Jesus prayer* is also known as *prayer of the heart*. In the heart is life, and precisely there in our heart we must learn to pray, "heart speaking to heart," breathing and praying the name of Jesus, the prayer of Jesus, the Heart of Jesus.

The usual form of the *Jesus prayer* is repetition of an invocation — for example, "Lord Jesus Christ, Son of God, have mercy on me a sinner." But Eastern spiritual masters also suggest varying the form by shortening it ("Lord Jesus, have mercy on me") or by lengthening it ("Lord Jesus Christ, Son of God, through the prayers of the Mother of God, have mercy on me a sinner") or by changing it to fit individual spiritual needs or preferences.

Although Pope John Paul has not specifically mentioned this, an appropriate result of personal reflections on the invocations of the Litany of the Heart of Jesus, under the direction of the Holy Father in these meditations, might be to discover appropriate invocations that touch the heart of one's personal union with the Lord Jesus and to use them as one's own personalized form of the *Jesus prayer*. Here are some examples:

"Heart of Jesus, propitiation for our sins, have mercy on me a sinner."

"Heart of Jesus, our life and resurrection, have mercy on me."

"Heart of Jesus, salvation of those who trust in you, have mercy on me in need of salvation."

For Pope John Paul II his favorite might be, "Heart of Jesus, fountain of life and holiness, have mercy on me."

Litany of the Sacred Heart

Lord, have mercy on us.
Christ, have mercy on us.
Lord, have mercy on us, Christ, hear us.
Christ, graciously hear us.
God the Father of heaven,
Have mercy on us.
God the Son, Redeemer of the world,
Have mercy on us.
God the Holy Spirit,
Have mercy on us.
Holy Trinity, one God,
Have mercy on us.

1. Heart of Jesus, Son of the eternal Father,
   [After each invocation the response is: *"Have mercy on us."*]
2. Heart of Jesus, formed by the Holy Spirit in the womb of the Virgin Mother,
3. Heart of Jesus, substantially united to the Word of God,
4. Heart of Jesus, of infinite majesty,
5. Heart of Jesus, sacred temple of God,
6. Heart of Jesus, tabernacle of the Most High,
7. Heart of Jesus, house of God and gate of heaven,
8. Heart of Jesus, burning furnace of charity,
9. Heart of Jesus, abode of justice and love,
10. Heart of Jesus, full of goodness and love,
11. Heart of Jesus, abyss of all virtues,

12. Heart of Jesus, most worthy of all praise,
13. Heart of Jesus, king and center of all hearts,
14. Heart of Jesus, in whom are all the treasures of wisdom and knowledge,
15. Heart of Jesus, in whom dwells the fullness of the divinity,
16. Heart of Jesus, in whom the Father was well pleased,
17. Heart of Jesus, of whose fullness we have all received,
18. Heart of Jesus, desire of the everlasting hills,
19. Heart of Jesus, patient and most merciful,
20. Heart of Jesus, enriching all who invoke you,
21. Heart of Jesus, fountain of life and holiness,
22. Heart of Jesus, propitiation for our sins,
23. Heart of Jesus, loaded down with opprobrium,
24. Heart of Jesus, bruised for our offenses,
25. Heart of Jesus, obedient unto death,
26. Heart of Jesus, pierced with a lance,
27. Heart of Jesus, source of all consolation,
28. Heart of Jesus, our life and resurrection,
29. Heart of Jesus, our peace and reconciliation,
30. Heart of Jesus, victim for sin,
31. Heart of Jesus, salvation of those who trust in you,
32. Heart of Jesus, hope of those who die in you,
33. Heart of Jesus, delight of all the saints,

Lamb of God, you take away the sins of the world,
Spare us, Lord.
Lamb of God, you take away the sins of the world,
Graciously hear us, O Lord.
Lamb of God, you take away the sins of the world,
Have mercy on us.
V. Jesus, meek and humble of heart.
R. Make our hearts like unto thine.

Let us pray:

Almighty and eternal God, look upon the Heart of your dearly beloved Son and upon the praise and satisfaction he offers you in the name of sinners, and being appeased, grant pardon to those who seek your mercy, in the name of the same Jesus Christ, your Son, who lives and reigns with you in the unity of the Holy Spirit, world without end. Amen.

Chronological list of Angelus messages

July 13, 1986	17	Heart of Jesus, of whose fullness we have all received
July 20, 1986	18	Heart of Jesus, desire of the everlasting hills
July 27, 1986	19	Heart of Jesus, patient and most merciful
August 3, 1986	20	Heart of Jesus, enriching all who invoke you
August 10, 1986	21	Heart of Jesus, fountain of life and holiness
August 17, 1986	22	Heart of Jesus, propitiation for our sins
August 24, 1986	23	Heart of Jesus, loaded down with opprobrium
August 31, 1986	24	Heart of Jesus, bruised for our offenses
July 2, 1989	2	Heart of Jesus, formed by the Holy Spirit in the womb of the Virgin Mother
July 9, 1989	3	Heart of Jesus, substantially united to the Word of God
July 23, 1989	25	Heart of Jesus, obedient unto death
July 30, 1989	26	Heart of Jesus, pierced with a lance
August 13, 1989	27	Heart of Jesus, source of all consolation
August 27, 1989	28	Heart of Jesus, our life and resurrection
September 3, 1989	29	Heart of Jesus, our peace and reconciliation
September 10, 1989	30	Heart of Jesus, victim for sin
September 17, 1989	31	Heart of Jesus, salvation of those who trust in you
November 5, 1989	32	Heart of Jesus, hope of those who die in you
November 12, 1989	33	Heart of Jesus, delight of all the saints

0

Litany of the Heart of Jesus reflects deepest experiences of human hearts

June 27, 1982

1 Heart of Jesus, formed by the Holy Spirit in the womb of the Virgin Mother, have mercy on us.

So we pray in the Litany of the Sacred Heart of Jesus.

This invocation refers directly to the mystery on which we meditate when we recite the Angelus: by the work of the Holy Spirit, there was formed in the womb of the Virgin of Nazareth the humanity of Christ, Son of the eternal Father.

By the work of the Holy Spirit, the Heart was formed in this humanity. The Heart, which is the central organ of Christ's human organism and at the same time the true symbol of his interior life: his thoughts, his will, his sentiments. Through this Heart, the humanity of Christ is in a particular way the "temple of God" and at the same time, through this Heart, it remains ever open to man and to everything human: "Heart of Jesus, of whose fullness we have all received."

2 The month of June is especially dedicated to the veneration of the divine Heart. Not just one day, the liturgical feast that usually falls in June, but every day. Connected with it is the devout practice of daily reciting or singing the Litany of the Sacred Heart of Jesus.

It is a marvelous prayer, totally concentrated on the interior mystery of Christ, the God-Man. The Litany to the Heart of Jesus draws abundantly from biblical sources, and at the same time reflects the deepest experiences of human hearts. It is also a prayer of veneration and authentic dialogue.

In it we speak of the heart, and we also allow our hearts to speak with this unique Heart that is the "source of life and holiness" and the "desire of the everlasting hills," with the Heart that is "patient and most merciful," enriching all who call upon him.

This prayer, recited and meditated, becomes a true school of the interior life, the school of the Christian.

3 The Solemnity of the Sacred Heart of Jesus reminds us above all of the moments when this Heart was "pierced with a lance" and by this piercing was visibly opened to man and to the world.

In reciting the Litany — and in venerating the divine Heart — we learn the mystery of redemption in all its divine and human depth.

At the same time we become sensitive to the need for reparation. Christ opens his Heart to us that we may join him in his reparation for the salvation of the world. The language of the pierced Heart speaks the whole truth about his gospel and about Easter.

Let us try to understand this language ever better. Let us learn it.

1

Heart of Jesus, Son of the eternal Father

June 2, 1985

1 Heart of Jesus, Son of the eternal Father.

Today, the first Sunday of the month of June, the Church finds in the Heart of Jesus access to the God who is the Holy Trinity, to the Father, the Son, and the Holy Spirit.

This one God — one and triune at the same time — is an ineffable mystery of faith.

Truly he "dwells in unapproachable light" (1 Timothy 6:16).

And at the same time the infinite God has allowed himself to be embraced by the Heart of that Man whose name is Jesus of Nazareth: Jesus Christ. And through the Heart of the Son, God the Father approaches our hearts and comes to them.

So each one of us has been baptized "in the name of the Father and of the Son and of the Holy Spirit." Each one of us has been, from the very beginning, immersed in the one and triune God: in the living God, in the life-giving God. This God we confess as the Holy Spirit who, proceeding from the Father and the Son, is "the giver of life."

2 The Heart of Jesus was "formed by the Holy Spirit in the womb of the Virgin Mother."

God who is "the giver of life," who "gives himself to man," began the work of his economy of salvation by becoming man.

Precisely in his virginal conception and birth from Mary

did his human Heart begin, "formed by the Holy Spirit in the womb of the Virgin Mother."

It is this Heart that we want to venerate during the month of June. This very day we want to make this Heart the fiduciary for our poor human hearts, hearts that are tried in various ways, oppressed in various ways, and at the same time hearts that are confident in the power of God himself and in the saving power of the Holy Trinity.

3 Mary, Virgin Mother, you better than we know the divine Heart of your Son. Join us in today's adoration of the Holy Trinity and in our humble prayer for the Church and for the world.

May you alone be the guide of this prayer of ours.

2

Heart of Jesus, formed by the Holy Spirit in the womb of the Virgin Mother

[Cf. No. 1, p. 25]

July 2, 1989

1 Exactly one month ago on June 2, we celebrated the Solemnity of the Sacred Heart of Jesus. I wish to resume meditating on the riches of this divine Heart, continuing our reflection on the Litany dedicated to it, which was begun in the past.

One of the most profound invocations of that Litany is the following: "Heart of Jesus, formed by the Holy Spirit in the womb of the Virgin Mother, have mercy on us." Here we find an echo of a central article of the Creed, in which we profess our faith in "Jesus Christ, the only Son of God," who "came down from heaven and by the power of the Holy Spirit became incarnate of the Virgin Mary and was made man." Therefore, Christ's sacred humanity is the work of the Holy Spirit and of the Virgin of Nazareth.

2 It is the work of the Spirit. The Evangelist Matthew states this explicitly, when referring to the angel's words to Joseph: "that which is conceived in her [Mary] is of the Holy Spirit" (Matthew 1:20). Similarly the evangelist Luke states it, recounting Gabriel's words to Mary: "The Holy Spirit will come upon you, and the power of the Most High will overshadow you" (1:35).

The Spirit shaped the sacred humanity of Christ: his body

and his soul with his intellect, will, and capacity to love. In a word, he molded his Heart. Christ's life was placed fully under the sign of the Spirit. From the Spirit there comes to him the wisdom which filled the doctors of the law and his fellow townspeople with amazement, the love which welcomes and pardons sinners, the mercy which stoops down to human misery, the tenderness which blesses and embraces the children, and the understanding which soothes the pain of the afflicted. It is the Spirit who directs the steps of Jesus, who sustains him in trials, and above all who guides him on his way to Jerusalem, where he will offer the sacrifice of the New Covenant, thanks to which the fire he brought to earth will be enkindled (Luke 12:49).

3 On the other hand, Christ's humanity is also the work of the Virgin. The Spirit molded the Heart of Jesus in the womb of Mary, who collaborated actively with him as mother and educator:

• As mother, she adhered knowingly and freely to the salvific plan of God the Father, accepting with trepidation and silent adoration the mystery of the life which had germinated and was developing in her;

• As educator, she had molded the Heart of her Son; with Saint Joseph she introduced him to the traditions of the Chosen People, inspired in him a love for the Law of the Lord, communicated to him the spirituality of the "poor of the Lord." She had helped him to develop his intellect and exercised a sure influence in the formation of his character. Although knowing that her Child surpassed her because he was "the Son of the Most High" (Luke 1:32), the Virgin was no less solicitous for his human upbringing (Luke 2:51).

Therefore we can truly say: in the Heart of Christ there shines forth the wonderful work of the Holy Spirit; in it there is also reflected the heart of his Mother. May every Christian heart be like the Heart of Christ: obedient to the Spirit's action and to the Mother's voice.

3

Heart of Jesus, substantially united to the Word of God

July 9, 1989

Heart of Jesus, substantially united to the Word of God, have mercy on us.

1 The expression "Heart of Jesus" immediately calls to mind Christ's humanity and emphasizes the wealth of his feelings: his compassion for the sick, his predilection for the poor, his mercy for sinners, his tenderness toward children, his strength in denouncing the hypocrisy of pride and violence, his meekness before his opponents, his zeal for the glory of the Father, and his rejoicing in the mysterious and providential plans of grace.

In referring to the facts of his passion, the expression "Heart of Jesus" also recalls Christ's sorrow over his betrayal by Judas, his distress due to loneliness, his anguish in the face of death, his filial and obedient abandonment into the hands of the Father. Most of all it speaks of the love which flows unceasingly from his inmost being: infinite love for the Father and limitless love for mankind.

2 Now this Heart which is humanly so rich "is united," as the invocation reminds us, to the Person of "the Word of God." Jesus is the incarnate Word of God: in him there is only one person, the eternal Person of the Word, subsisting in two natures, divine and human. Jesus is one in the indivisible reality of his being and, at the same time, perfect in his divinity, perfect in our humanity. He is equal to the Father in all that concerns his divine nature, equal to us in all that concerns the human nature: true Son of God and true Son of man. The Heart of Jesus, therefore, from the very moment of his incarnation has been and will always be united to the Person of the Word of God.

Through the union of the Heart of Jesus to the Person of the Word of God we can say that in Jesus, God loves humanly, suffers in a human manner, and rejoices in a human way. And vice versa, in Jesus human love, human suffering, and human glory acquire a divine intensity and power.

3 Dear brothers and sisters, gathered for the prayer of the Angelus, let us contemplate with Mary the Heart of Christ. The Virgin lived in faith day after day at the side of her Son, Jesus; she knew that the flesh of her Son came from her virginal flesh, but she understood that because he was the "Son of the Most High" (Luke 1:32), he infinitely transcended her. The Heart of her Son was in fact "united to the Person of the Word." Therefore she loved him as her Son and at the same time adored him as her Lord and God. May she grant us also to love and adore Christ, God and Man, above all things, with all our hearts, all our souls, and all our minds (Matthew 22:37). In such a way, following her example, we will be the object of the special divine and human love of the Heart of her Son.

4

Heart of Jesus, of infinite majesty

June 16, 1985

1 Through the immaculate heart of Mary we desire to turn to the divine Heart of her Son, to the Heart of Jesus of infinite majesty.

Behold, the infinite majesty of God is hidden in the human Heart of the Son of Mary.

This Heart is our covenant!

This Heart is the greatest proximity to God as regards human hearts and human history.

This Heart is the wonderful "condescension" of God: the human Heart which pulsates with divine life, the divine life which pulsates in the human heart.

2 In the Holy Eucharist we discover "with the sense of faith" the same Heart:

• Heart of infinite majesty which continues to pulsate with the human love of Christ the God-Man.

How profoundly Pope Saint Pius X, former patriarch of Venice, felt this love:

• How greatly he desired that all Christians from childhood on should approach the Eucharist through Holy Communion, so as to unite themselves to that Heart which, at the same time, is for every person "house of God and gate of heaven."

"House," yes; through Eucharistic communion the Heart of Jesus offers a dwelling place for every human heart.

"Gate," yes, for in each of these human hearts he opens the perspective of the eternal union with the Holy Trinity.

3 Mother of God! While we meditate on the mystery of your annunciation, draw us close to this divine Heart. . .
- Heart of infinite majesty,
- House of God and gate of heaven,

. . .this Heart which from the moment of the angel's word began to beat close to your virginal and maternal heart.

5

Heart of Jesus, sacred temple of God

June 9, 1985

1 At the moment of our common prayer of the Angelus, we turn, together with Mary — through her immaculate heart — to the divine Heart of her Son: "Heart of Jesus, sacred temple of God, Heart of Jesus, tabernacle of the Most High."

Heart of a man similar to so very many other human hearts and, at the same time, Heart of God the Son.

If therefore it is true that every man "dwells" in some sense in his heart, then in the Heart of the Man of Nazareth, of Jesus Christ, God dwells. It is the "temple of God," being the Heart of this Man.

2 God the Son is united with the Father as the eternal Word: "God from God, Light from Light . . . generated not created."

The Son is united with the Father in the Holy Spirit, who is the "breath" of the Father and the Son and in the divine Trinity is the Love-Person.

The Heart of the Man Jesus Christ is therefore, in the trinitarian sense, the "temple of God": it is the interior temple of the Son who is united with the Father in the Holy Spirit by means of the unity of the divinity. How inscrutable is the mystery of this Heart which is the "temple of God" and the "tabernacle of the Most High."

3 At the same time it is the true "dwelling place of God with men" (Revelation 21:3) because the Heart of Jesus in its interior temple embraces all men. All dwell there, embraced by eternal love. To all — in the Heart of Jesus — can be applied the words of the prophet: "I have loved you with an everlasting love, therefore I have continued my faithfulness to you" (Jeremiah 31:3).

4 May this power of eternal love which is in the divine Heart of Jesus be communicated today in a special way to the young people who received Confirmation.

In them the Holy Spirit should dwell in a special way.

May their hearts also become like that of Christ "a holy temple of God" and a "tabernacle of the Most High."

I have often heard young people sing: "Do you know that you are a temple?" Yes. We are the temple of God and the Spirit of God dwells in us, according to the words of Saint Paul (1 Corinthians 3:16).

5 Through the immaculate heart of Mary, let us remain in the covenant with the Heart of Jesus who is the "temple of God," the most splendid "tabernacle of the Most High" and the most perfect.

6

Heart of Jesus, tabernacle of the Most High

[Cf. No. 5, p. 33]

7

Heart of Jesus, house of God and gate of heaven

[Cf. No. 4, p. 31]

8

Heart of Jesus, burning furnace of charity

June 23, 1985

1 Heart of Jesus, burning furnace of charity.

During the Angelus we desire, together with the Mother of God, to turn our hearts to the Heart of her divine Son.

The invocations of this splendid Litany, which we recite or sing especially during the month of June, speak to us profoundly. May the Mother help us understand better the mysteries of the Heart of her Son.

2 "Furnace of charity." A furnace burns and, in burning, it consumes everything, be it wood or other easily combustible substances.

The Heart of Jesus, the human Heart of Jesus, burns with love which fills it; and this is love for the eternal Father and love for mankind, for his adopted sons and daughters.

The burning furnace gradually spends itself. The Heart of Jesus, on the other hand, is an inextinguishable furnace. In this it resembles the "burning bush" in the Book of Exodus, in which God revealed himself to Moses. The bush which burned in the fire, yet . . . "it was not consumed" (Exodus 3:2).

In fact, the love which burns in the Heart of Jesus is above all the Holy Spirit, in which the God-Son is united eternally with the Father. The Heart of Jesus, the human Heart of the God-Man, is embraced by the "living flame" of trinitarian love which is never extinguished.

3 Heart of Jesus, burning furnace of charity. The furnace as it burns illumines the darkness of the night and warms the bodies of the frozen wayfarers.

Today we pray to the Mother of the eternal Word that on the horizon of the life of each one of us the Heart of Jesus may never cease to burn — burning furnace of charity. That it may reveal to us the love which is never extinguished and never diminishes, the love which is eternal. That it may illuminate the darkness of the earthly night and warm our hearts.

4 How the Church is gladdened by the fact that through this divine Heart, human hearts burn with love. How the Church rejoices today that such love enkindled the heart of Father Benedetto Menni, priest of the Hospitallers of Saint John of God and founder of the Congregation of the Hospitaller Sisters of the Sacred Heart of Jesus; and the heart of Brother Peter Friedhofen, layman and founder of the Brothers of Mercy of Mary Auxiliatrix.

5 In expressing gratitude for the only love capable of transforming the world and human life, let us turn with the immaculate Virgin at the moment of the annunciation to the divine Heart which does not cease to be a "burning furnace of charity," burning like that "bush" which Moses saw at the foot of Mount Horeb.

[For more on this invocation, see No. 10, Part 4, p. 46]

9

Heart of Jesus, abode of justice and love

June 30, 1985

1 Heart of Jesus, abode of justice and love.

From the center of our assembly gathered here on the concluding day of the Eucharistic Congress in Teramo, we pray, as always at this hour, the Angelus.

Let us reflect together with the Virgin of Nazareth on the moment of the annunciation.

Let us reflect on the mystery of the incarnation.

"The Word was made flesh and dwelt among us" (John 1:14); in fact, he came to live in the womb of Mary, beneath her heart.

2 Between the heart of the Mother and the Heart of the Child (her Son) there was from the very beginning a bond, a splendid union of hearts. The heart of Mary is the first to speak to the Heart of Jesus. The first, one can say, to recite the Litany to this Heart.

Let us unite ourselves to her.

3 Heart of Jesus, abode of justice: in you the eternal Father offered humanity the justice which abides in the Holy Trinity, in God himself. Justice which is from God constitutes the definitive foundation of our justification.

This justice comes to us through love. Christ loved us and gave himself for us (Galatians 2:20). And, indeed, with this giving of himself through a love more powerful than death, he has justified us. He "was raised for our justification" (Romans 4:25).

4 At this hour of the Angelus the Eucharistic Congress of Teramo prays, professing together with the Mother of God the mysteries of the Sacred Heart of Jesus.

These mysteries expressed so beautifully in the invocations of the Litany guide us along the ways of our earthly life to the eternal home of the divine Heart, where God will wipe away all tears from our eyes (Revelation 7:17; 21:4).

When he himself will be "everything to everyone" (1 Corinthians 15:28).

July 14, 1985

1 Heart of Jesus, "abode of justice and love."

The Angelus reminds us every time of that salvific moment when, under the heart of the Virgin of Nazareth, the Heart of the Word, the Son of God, began to beat. In her womb he became man through the action of the Holy Spirit. In Mary's womb the Man was conceived, and the Heart was conceived.

2 This Heart, like every human heart, is a center, an abode in which the spiritual life beats with a special rhythm: the heart, irreplaceable echo of all that tests the human spirit.

Every human heart is called to beat with a rhythm of justice and love. From it is measured the true dignity of man.

3 The Heart of Jesus beats with a rhythm of justice and love according to the same divine measure. It is precisely the Heart of the God-Man. In him all God's justice toward man must ultimately be fulfilled, and also in a certain sense man's justice toward God. In the human Heart of the Son of God is offered to mankind the justice of God himself.

This justice is at the same time the gift of love.

Through the Heart of Jesus love enters into the history of mankind as subsistent love: "God so loved the world that he gave his only Son" (John 3:16).

4 We desire to fix our gaze, with the eyes of the immaculate Virgin, on the light of that admirable mystery, the justice which is revealed as love, love which fills to the brim every measure of justice and goes beyond it.

Let us pray: Through your heart, O Mother of God, may the Heart of Jesus as "abode of justice and love" become for all of us "the way, the truth, and the life."

10

Heart of Jesus, full of goodness and love

July 21, 1985

1 Heart of Jesus, full of goodness and love.

In our Angelus we wish to turn our thoughts to the Heart of Christ, following the words of the Litany.

We wish to speak to the Heart of the Son through the heart of the Mother. What can be more beautiful than the colloquy of these two hearts? We now wish to share in it.

2 The Heart of Jesus is a "burning furnace of charity," for charity has something of the nature of fire which burns and blazes in order to illuminate and to warm.

At the same time, in the sacrifice of Calvary the Redeemer's Heart was not destroyed by the fire of suffering. Even if it was humanly dead, as the Roman centurion ensured by piercing Christ's side with a lance, in the divine plan of salvation this Heart remains alive, as the resurrection has manifested.

3 And so, the living Heart itself of the risen and glorified Redeemer is "full of goodness and love," infinitely and superabundantly overflowing. In Christ the overflowing of the human heart attains the divine measure.

Such was this Heart already during the days of his earthly life. What is narrated in the gospel bears witness to it. The fullness of charity manifests itself through goodness: through goodness it shone and diffused itself on all — first of all on the suffering and the poor, on all according to their need and their truest expectations.

Such is the human Heart of God's Son also after the experience of the cross and of the sacrifice. Even more, it is full of love and goodness.

4 At the moment of the annunciation the colloquy of the Mother's heart with the Heart of the Son began. Today we join in this colloquy by meditating on the mystery of the incarnation in the Angelus.

11

Heart of Jesus, abyss of all virtues

July 28, 1985

Heart of Jesus, abyss of all virtues.

1 Under the Mother's heart the Man was conceived. The Son of God was conceived as man. To venerate the moment of this conception, the mystery of the incarnation, we join in the prayer of the Angelus.

In the light of the moment of the conception, in the light of the mystery of the incarnation, we look at the whole life of Jesus, born of Mary. Following the invocations of the Litany, we seek to describe in some way this inner life, by means of his Heart.

2 The heart determines the depth of the person. In every case it indicates the extent of this depth, whether in the interior experience of each one of us or also in interpersonal communication. The depth of Jesus Christ, indicated by the measure of his Heart, is peerless. It surpasses the depth of any person whatsoever, because it is not merely human but at the same time divine.

3 This divine-human depth of the Heart of Jesus is the depth of the virtues, of all the virtues. As a true man Jesus expresses the interior language of his Heart by means of the virtues. In fact, by analyzing his conduct, all these virtues can be discovered and identified, as historically they proceed from human moral consciousness as the cardinal virtues (prudence, justice, fortitude, temperance) and the others derived from them. (These virtues were possessed in a high degree by the saints and, always with divine grace, by the great exponents of human moral standards.)

4 The invocations of the Litany speak in a very beautiful way of an "abyss" of the virtues of Jesus. This abyss, this depth, signifies a special degree of perfection of each of the virtues and its precise power. This depth and power of each virtue proceeds from love. The more all the virtues are rooted in love, the greater is their depth.

In addition to love, we must add that humility too determines the depth of the virtues. Jesus said: "Learn of me for I am gentle and lowly in heart" (Matthew 11:29).

5 In reciting the Angelus let us ask Mary that we may ever draw closer to the Heart of her Son, so that we may be enabled to learn from him and from his virtues.

12

Heart of Jesus, most worthy of all praise

August 4, 1985

1 We meet again, dear brothers and sisters, to reverence that unique moment in the history of the universe in which God the Son became man beneath the heart of the Virgin of Nazareth.

It is the moment of the annunciation which the Angelus reflects: "Behold you will conceive and bear a son and you shall call his name Jesus. He will be called the Son of the Most High" (Luke 1:31-32).

Mary said: "Let it be to me according to your word" (Luke 1:38).

And from that moment her heart prepared itself to welcome the God-Man: "Heart of Jesus, most worthy of all praise."

2 Let us join the Mother of God to adore this Heart of the Man which, through the mystery of the hypostatic union (union of the natures), is at the same time the Heart of God.

Let us render to God the adoration owed to the Heart of Jesus Christ from the first moment of his conception in the Virgin's womb.

Together with Mary let us render the same adoration at the moment of the birth, when he comes into the world in the extreme poverty of Bethlehem. Together with Mary let us render the same adoration to him through all the days and years of his hidden life at Nazareth, through all the days and years in which he fulfilled his messianic service in Israel.

And when the time of the passion arrives, the time of the stripping, of the humiliation, and of the opprobrium of the cross, let us unite ourselves still more ardently with the Mother's heart to cry out: "Heart of Jesus, most worthy of all praise."

Yes, most worthy of all praise precisely because of this opprobrium and humiliation! In fact, the Redeemer's Heart then reaches the summit of God's love.

And precisely Love is worthy of all praise!

For us "let there not be any other boast but in the cross of the Lord Jesus Christ" (Galatians 6:14), Saint Paul wrote, while Saint John teaches, "God is love" (1 John 4:8).

3 Jesus Christ is in the glory of God the Father. With this glory, in the Holy Spirit, the Father surrounds the Heart of his glorified Son. This glory proclaims down the centuries the assumption into heaven of the heart of his Mother. Let all of us join with her to profess: "Heart of Jesus, most worthy of all praise, have mercy on us."

13

Heart of Jesus, king and center of all hearts

August 25, 1985

1 Heart of Jesus, king and center of all hearts.

Jesus Christ is king of hearts. We know that during his messianic activity in Palestine the people, seeing the signs that he had performed, wanted to proclaim him king.

They saw in Christ a true descendant of David, during whose reign Israel was at the height of its splendor.

2 We know that before the tribunal of Pilate, when asked, "Are you a king?" Jesus of Nazareth replied: "My kingship is not of this world. . . . For this I was born and for this I have come into the world, to bear witness to the truth. Everyone who is of the truth hears my voice" (John 18:33, 36-37).

3 In this manner Christ is king of hearts. He never desired to be a temporal ruler, not even on the throne of David.

He desired only that kingship which is not of this world and which, at the same time, is rooted in this world by way of truth in human hearts, in the inner man.

For this kingship he announced the gospel and performed great signs. For this kingship, the kingdom of adopted sons and daughters of God, he gave his life on the cross.

4 He reconfirmed this kingship with his resurrection, giving the Holy Spirit to the apostles and to the people in the Church.

In this manner Jesus Christ is the king and center of all hearts.

Reunited in him by truth we draw near to one another in the union of the kingdom in which God "will wipe away every tear" (Revelation 7:17) because he will be "everything to everyone" (1 Corinthians 15:28).

5 Joined together today for our usual Angelus, let us, together with the Mother of God, invoke the Heart of her Son: "Heart of Jesus, king and center of all hearts, have mercy on me."

Immaculate heart of Mary, guide our prayer, which today is full of thanks to the Lord for my recent apostolic journey to Africa [August 8-19].

14

Heart of Jesus, in whom are all the treasures of wisdom and knowledge

September 1, 1985

1 Heart of Jesus, in whom are all the treasures of wisdom and knowledge.

This invocation from the Litany of the Sacred Heart, based on a text from the letter to the Colossians (2:3), permits us to understand the necessity of going to the Heart of Christ to enter into the fullness of God.

2 The knowledge referred to here is not the knowledge that "puffs up" (1 Corinthians 8:1), knowledge based on human ability. It is divine wisdom, a mystery hidden for centuries in the mind of God, Creator of the universe (Ephesians 3:9). It is a new knowledge, hidden from the wise and learned but revealed to little ones (Matthew 11:25), those who are rich in humility, simplicity, and purity of heart.

This knowledge and wisdom consist in recognizing the mystery of the invisible God who calls men to share in his divine nature and admits them into communion with himself.

3 We know these things because God himself has deigned to reveal them to us through his Son, who is the wisdom of God (1 Corinthians 1:24).

All things in heaven and on earth were created through him and for him (Colossians 1:16). The wisdom of Christ is greater than that of Solomon (Luke 11:31). His riches are unsearchable (Ephesians 3:8). His love surpasses all knowledge. With faith, however, we are able to comprehend with all the saints what is the breadth, length, height, and depth (Ephesians 3:18).

Knowing Jesus, we also know God. Whoever sees him sees the Father (John 14:9). With him the love of God has been poured into our hearts (Romans 5:5).

4 Human knowledge is like water from our wells; whoever drinks it will thirst again. The wisdom and knowledge of Jesus, however, open the eyes of the mind, stir the heart in the depths of its being, and arouse man to transcendent love; they liberate him from the darkness of error, from the stain of sin, from the danger of death, and lead him to the full sharing of those divine benefits, which surpass the powers of the human mind to understand (*Dei Verbum,* No. 6).

5 With the wisdom and knowledge of Jesus, we are rooted and grounded in charity (Ephesians 3:17). A new, interior man is created, one who puts God at the center of his own life and himself at the service of his brothers.

This is the degree of perfection which Mary reaches, the Mother of Jesus and our Mother, the only example of a new creature enriched with the fullness of grace and ready to do the will of God: "Behold the handmaid of the Lord, be it done to me according to your word." For this reason we invoke her as "Seat of wisdom."

Reciting the Angelus, we ask her to make us like herself and like her Son.

15

Heart of Jesus, in whom dwells the fullness of the divinity

September 15, 1985

1 Heart of Jesus, in whom dwells the fullness of the divinity.
Beginning in the month of June and continuing throughout the summer months, our praying of the Angelus has been joined with some reflection on the Litany of the Sacred Heart of Jesus.

We pause to dwell upon an individual invocation and to meditate on the great richness of the contents included in it. It is a source of inspiration for our interior life and for our understanding of the mystery of Jesus Christ.

2 Yesterday, on the Solemnity of the Triumph of the Holy Cross the whole Church opened itself once again to this Heart in whom "dwells the fullness of the divinity."

The mystery of Christ, the God-Man, has a particular eloquence when we look at the cross: Behold the Man! Behold the Crucified! Behold the Man totally despoiled! Behold the Man "broken for our sins," behold the Man "covered with opprobrium."

And at the same time, behold the Man-God! In him dwells the fullness of the divinity. Consubstantial with the Father! God from God! Light from Light! Begotten not made! The Eternal Word! One in divinity with the Father and the Holy Spirit.

3 When on Golgotha the centurion pierced the Crucified with a lance, blood and water poured forth from his side. This is a sign of death, the sign of the human death of the immortal God.

4 At the foot of the cross was his Mother, the sorrowful
Mother. We remember her especially on the day after the
triumph of the cross. When the side of Christ was pierced with
the centurion's lance, Simeon's prophecy was fulfilled in her:
"And a sword will pierce through your own soul also" (Luke
2:35).

The words of the prophet are a foretelling of the definitive
alliance of these hearts: of the Son and of the Mother, of the
Mother and of the Son. "Heart of Jesus, in whom dwells all the
fullness of the divinity." Heart of Mary, heart of the sorrowful
Virgin, heart of the Mother of God!

May our prayer of the Angelus unite us today with that
admirable alliance of hearts.

June 15, 1986

**[In Part 4 of his Angelus homily of June 15, 1986, the
Holy Father adverted briefly to this same invocation as
follows:]**

4 Let us proclaim during this month of June the words of the
Litany:

Heart of Jesus, in whom dwells the fullness of the divinity.
Heart of Jesus, of whose fullness we have all received.

Let us unite in this prayer with Mary, who better than
anyone else knows this "fullness" and knows how to draw from
it more fully

16

Heart of Jesus, in whom the Father was well pleased

June 22, 1986

1 Heart of Jesus, in whom the Father was well pleased.

Praying in this way, especially now in the month of June, let us meditate on the eternal satisfaction which the Father has in the Son, God in God, Light in Light.

This satisfaction means love, this love to which everything that exists owes its being. Without it, without love, and without the Word-Son "was not anything made that was made" (John 1:3).

This satisfaction of the Father found its manifestation in the work of creation, especially in the creation of man, when "God saw everything that he had made, and behold, it was good, it was very good" (Genesis 1:31).

Is not the Heart of Jesus then the "point" in which the human person can regain full confidence in all that is created? He sees the values, the order, and the beauty of the world. He sees the meaning of life.

2 Heart of Jesus, in whom the Father was well pleased.

Let us go to the bank of the Jordan.

Let us go to Mount Tabor.

In both of these events described by the evangelists the voice of the invisible God is heard, and it is the voice of the Father: "This is my beloved Son, with whom I am well pleased; listen to him" (Matthew 17:5).

The eternal satisfaction of the Father accompanied the Son when he became man, when he accepted the messianic mission to be carried out in the world, when he said that his food was to do the Father's will.

Christ fulfilled this will to the end, making himself obedient even to death on the cross, and so that eternal satisfaction of the Father in the Son, which belongs to the intimate mystery of the triune God, has become part of the history of humanity. The Son himself became man, and as such he had a human Heart, with which he loved and responded to love, first of all to the Father's love.

Therefore on this Heart, on the Heart of Jesus, the Father's satisfaction is concentrated.

It is a salvific satisfaction. Through it the Father embraces, in the Heart of his Son, everyone for whom this Son became man, everyone for whom he has a heart, everyone for whom he died and rose.

In the Heart of Jesus mankind and the world rediscover the Father's satisfaction. This is the Heart of our Redeemer; it is the Heart of the Redeemer of the world.

3 Let us unite with Mary in our recitation of the Angelus.

Let us unite with her, from whom the Son of God received a human Heart. Let us pray that she may lead us closer to that Heart. Let us pray that she, in the Heart of the Son, may bring the Father's satisfaction, the Father's love, God's mercy, closer to mankind and to the world.

17

Heart of Jesus, of whose fullness we have all received

July 13, 1986

1 Heart of Jesus, of whose fullness we have all received.
Gathered to recite the Angelus, we unite with Mary in the moment of the annunciation when the Word was made flesh and came to dwell "beneath her heart," the heart of the Mother.

Let us unite then with the heart of the Mother, who from the moment of his conception best knew the human Heart of her divine Son: "Of his fullness we have all received, grace upon grace," as the evangelist John wrote (1:16).

2 What determines the fullness of the heart? When can we say that the heart is full? With what is the Heart of Jesus filled?
It is filled with love.

Love determines this fullness of the Heart of the Son of God to which we turn today in prayer.

It is a Heart filled with love of the Father, filled in both a divine and a human way. In fact the Heart of Jesus is truly the human Heart of the God-Son. It is filled with filial love: all that he did and said on earth gives testimony to his filial love.

3 At the same time the filial love of the Heart of Jesus has revealed, and continually reveals to the world, the love of the Father. The Father has "loved the world so much that he gave his only-begotten Son" (John 3:16) for the salvation of the world, for the salvation of man, so that he "should not die, but have eternal life" (ibid.).

The Heart of Jesus is therefore full of love for man. It is full of love for the creature, full of love for the world.

How full it is! This fullness is never exhausted.

When humanity draws on the material resources of the land, water, and air, these resources diminish and little by little are exhausted.

We often speak of the rapidly expanding exploitation of these resources taking place today. From this come warnings, such as "we must not overexploit."

But love is an entirely different matter. The fullness of the Heart of Jesus is another matter.

It is never exhausted, nor will it ever be exhausted.

Of this fullness we have all received grace upon grace. We only need to enlarge our hearts, our openness to receive this superabundance of love.

For this very reason we unite ourselves with the heart of Mary.

[Cf. also Part 4 of the Holy Father's Angelus homily for June 15, 1986, appended to No. 15 on p. 56]

18

Heart of Jesus, desire of the everlasting hills

July 20, 1986

1 Heart of Jesus, desire of the everlasting hills.

In the course of these Sundays, as we gather for noon prayer, we recite the Litany of the Sacred Heart in special union with the Mother of Jesus.

The Sunday Angelus is, in fact, our appointment for prayer with Mary. Together with her we recall the annunciation, which was certainly a decisive event in her life.

Behold, at the center of this event we find the Heart. We are speaking of the love of the Son of God, which from the moment of his incarnation, began to develop "beneath the heart" of the Mother along with the human Heart of her Son.

2 Is this Heart the "desire" of the world?

Observing the world as it visibly surrounds us, we must note with Saint John that it is subjected to the lust of the flesh and the lust of the eyes and the pride of life (1 John 2:16), and this "world" seems to be far removed from the desire of the Heart of Jesus. It does not share his desires. It remains extraneous and at times directly hostile to them.

This is the "world" which the Council says is "subject to the slavery of sin" (*Gaudium et Spes*, No. 2). It says this in conformity with the whole of revelation, the Scriptures, and Tradition (and finally, we should say, with our human experience).

3 Yet, at the same time the same "world" is called into existence by the love of the Creator and by this love it is constantly maintained in existence. We are speaking here of the world composed of visible and invisible creatures and in particular of the "entire human family in the context of all the realities in which it lives" (*Gaudium et Spes*, No. 2).

It is the world which, because of its "slavery to sin," is subject to corruption, as Saint Paul teaches, and therefore groans and suffers in travail, awaiting with eager longing the revealing of the sons of God, for only in such a way can it be truly liberated from the slavery of corruption to participate in freedom and in the glory of the sons of God (Romans 8:19-22).

4 This world, despite sin and its triple concupiscence, is directed toward the love which fills the human Heart of the Son of Mary.

Therefore, in union with her we ask: Heart of Jesus, desire of the everlasting hills, bring to human hearts, bring to our times that liberation which is in your gospel, in your cross and resurrection: the liberation which is in your Heart.

19

Heart of Jesus, patient and most merciful

July 27, 1986

1 Heart of Jesus, patient and most merciful.

Today, on the occasion of the Angelus, we desire, together with Mary, to reread the gospel once again; in a certain sense, we are rereading it in its entirety and all at once. In it is inscribed the Heart of Jesus, patient and most merciful.

Is it not perhaps the Heart of him who "went about doing good" to all (Acts 10:38)? Of him who made the blind receive their sight, the lame walk, the dead to be raised up, and the poor to have the good news preached to them (Luke 7:22)?

Is it not perhaps the Heart of Jesus who himself had no place to rest his head, while the foxes have their dens and the birds their nests (Matthew 8:20)?

Is it not perhaps the Heart of Jesus who defended the adulterous woman from stoning and then said to her: "Go and sin no more" (John 8:3-10)?

Is it not perhaps the Heart of Jesus who was called "friend of publicans and sinners" (Matthew 11:19)?

2 Together with Mary, let us look into this Heart!

Let us reread it in the entire gospel.

Most of all, let us reread this Heart in the moment of the crucifixion, when it was pierced by the lance, when the mystery written in it was completely revealed.

The patient Heart, because it is open to all the sufferings of man. The patient Heart, because it is itself disposed to accept a suffering beyond any human measure.

The patient Heart, because it is most merciful.

What really is mercy, if it is not that very special measure of love which is expressed in suffering?

What really is mercy, if not that definitive measure of love which descends into the very center of evil to overcome it with good?

What is it, if not the love which overcomes the sin of the world through suffering and death?

3 Heart of Jesus, patient and most merciful.

Mother, present beneath the cross, you looked into his Heart!

Mother, by the will of this Heart, you have become Mother to us all.

Who knows the mystery of the Heart of Jesus like you — at Bethlehem, Nazareth, and Calvary?

Who else but you knows that it is patient and most merciful?

Who like you bears such unending witness to it?

20

Heart of Jesus, enriching all who invoke you

August 3, 1986

1 Heart of Jesus, enriching all who invoke you.

We gather today during the Angelus to recall, O Mother of Christ, the event that took place at Cana of Galilee.

This occurred at the beginning of his messianic activity. Jesus, along with you and his first disciples, was invited to the marriage. And when the wine ran out, Mary, you said to Jesus, "[Son,] they have no wine" (John 2:3).

You knew his Heart. You knew that it enriches all who invoke it.

With your prayer at Cana of Galilee you caused the Heart of Jesus to reveal his generosity.

2 This is the generous Heart, because fullness abides in it: in Christ, true Man, abides the fullness of the divinity; and God is Love.

He is generous because he loves, and to love means to expand, to give. To love means to be a gift. It means to be for others, to be for all, to be for each person.

For each person who calls: calls sometimes even without words, calls by the fact that puts the naked truth in plain light, and in this truth calls forth love.

Truth has the strength to call forth love. Through the truth all those who are poor in spirit, who hunger and thirst for justice, who are themselves merciful, have the strength to call forth love.

All of those, and many others as well, have a marvelous

"power" over love. All cause love to communicate itself, to give itself, and thus to manifest generosity of heart.

Among all of these, O Mary, you are the first.

3 Heart of Jesus, enriching all who invoke you.

Love will never be depleted through this generosity but will grow. It grows continuously, such is the mysterious nature of love. And such also is the mystery of the Heart of Jesus, enriching all.

It is open for each and every person. It is completely open of itself. Its generosity will never be depleted. The generosity of the Heart of Jesus gives testimony to the fact that love is not subject to the laws of death but to the laws of resurrection and life. It gives witness to the fact that love grows with love, such is its very nature.

4 In our time, Paul VI bore testimony to this truth about love. His human heart stopped beating here at Castel Gandolfo, eight years ago [August 6, 1978] on the Feast of the Transfiguration of the Lord.

His humble successor makes his own the same truth about love which the deceased Pontiff proclaimed by his word and by his life to the very end, invoking the divine Heart.

Thus, thinking of Paul VI today, during the prayer of the Angelus, we unite in a special way with Mary and pray: Heart of Jesus, enriching all who invoke you, receive your servant into your eternal light.

21

Heart of Jesus, fountain of life and holiness

August 10, 1986

1 Heart of Jesus, fountain of life and holiness.
Fountain!
We recall when Jesus went to the village of Samaria, Sichar, where there was a well that dated back to the time of the patriarch Jacob.

There he met a Samaritan woman who had come to draw water from the well. He said to her: "Give me a drink." The woman replied: "How is it that you, a Jew, ask a drink of me, a woman of Samaria?"

Then Jesus replied: "If you knew the gift of God and who it is that is saying to you 'Give me a drink' you would have asked him, and he would have given you living water."

He continued: "the water that I shall give will become a spring of water welling up to eternal life" (John 4:5-14).

Fountain. Fountain of life and holiness.

2 On another occasion, on the last day of the Festival of Booths in Jerusalem, Jesus, as once again John writes, "exclaimed in a loud voice: 'If any one thirst, let him come to me and drink. He who believes in me, as the Scripture has said, "Out of his heart shall flow rivers of living water." ' " The Evangelist added: "Now this he said about the Spirit, which those who believed in him were to receive" (John 7:37-39).

3 We all desire to draw near to this fountain of living water We all desire to drink from the divine Heart which is the fountain of life and holiness.

In it we are given the Holy Spirit, who is constantly given to all who draw near to Christ, to his Heart, with adoration and love.

To draw near to the fountain means to arrive at the source. There is no other place in the created world from which we can draw holiness in human life other than in his Heart, which has loved so much. "Springs of living water" have welled up in so many hearts and continue to do so today. The saints of all ages bear witness to it.

4 We ask you, Mother of Christ, be our guide to the Heart of your Son. We pray to you, lead us close to him and teach us to live in intimacy with this Heart, which is the fountain of life and holiness.

22

Heart of Jesus, propitiation for our sins

August 17, 1986

1 Heart of Jesus, propitiation for our sins.

The Heart of Jesus is the fountain of life, because through it victory over death is realized. It is the fountain of holiness, because in it sin, the adversary of holiness in the human heart, is overcome.

Jesus, who on the day of the resurrection comes through the locked doors of the Cenacle, says to his apostles: "Receive the Holy Spirit, whose sins you shall forgive, they shall be forgiven them" (John 20:23).

Saying this, he shows them his hands and side where the marks of the crucifixion are visible. He shows them his side where his Heart was pierced by the centurion's lance.

2 Thus the apostles were called to return to the Heart of Jesus, which is propitiation for the sins of the world. We too are called with them.

The power to forgive sins, the power of victory over evil which resides in the human heart, is contained in the passion and death of Christ our Redeemer. His Heart is a special sign of this redeeming power.

The passion and death of Christ involved his whole body. They were effected through all the wounds which he received during the passion. However, they were above all accomplished in his Heart, because it agonized in the dying of his entire body. His Heart was consumed in the throbbing pain of all his wounds.

3 In this despoliation the Heart burned with love; a living fire of love consumed the Heart of Jesus on the cross.

This love of the Heart was the propitiating power for sins. It overcame and overcomes for all time all the evil contained in sin, all estrangement from God, all rebellion of the human free will, all improper use of created freedom which opposes God and his holiness.

The love which consumed the Heart of Jesus, the love which caused the death of his Heart, was and is an invincible power. Through the love of the divine Heart, death brought victory over sin and became the fountain of life and holiness.

4 Christ himself knows the depth of the saving mystery of his Heart. He is the immediate witness to it. When he says to the apostles: "Receive the Holy Spirit for the remission of sins," he renders testimony to that heart which is propitiation for the sins of the world.

Mary, refuge of sinners, draw us near to the heart of your Son!

23

Heart of Jesus, loaded down with opprobrium

August 24, 1986

1 Heart of Jesus, loaded down with opprobrium.

These words from the Litany of the Sacred Heart help us to reread the gospel of the passion of Christ.

With the eyes of our spirit, let us pass through these moments and events, from the arrest in Gethsemane, to the judgment before Annas and Caiphas, his night in prison, the morning sentence of the Sanhedrin, the tribunal of the Roman governor, the tribunal of Herod the Galilean, the flagellation, the crowning with thorns, the sentence of crucifixion, the way of the cross to Golgotha, and finally, through his agony on the tree of ignominy, until the last "It is finished."

Heart of Jesus, loaded down with opprobrium.

2 Heart of Jesus, human Heart of the Son of God, so conscious of the dignity of every person, so conscious of the dignity of the God-Man.

Heart of the Son, firstborn of all creation, so conscious of the special dignity of the human soul and body, so sensitive to everything that offends this dignity: "loaded down with opprobrium."

3 Listen to the words of Isaiah the prophet: "Behold my servant, whom I uphold, my chosen, in whom my soul delights. . . . He will bring forth justice to the nations. . ." (42:1).

"He will not cry or lift up his voice . . . a bruised reed he will not break, and a dimly burning wick he will not quench. . ." (Isaiah 42:2-3).

"As many were astonished at him — his appearance was so marred, beyond human semblance, and his form beyond that of the sons of men" (Isaiah 52:14).

"A man of sorrow, and acquainted with grief, and as one from whom men hide their faces he was despised, and we esteemed him not" (Isaiah 53:3).

4 Heart of Jesus, loaded down with opprobrium.

Heart of Jesus, loaded down with opprobrium, a sign of contradiction.

"And a sword will pierce through your own soul also," Mary (Luke 2:35).

24

Heart of Jesus, bruised for our offenses

August 31, 1986

1 Heart of Jesus, bruised for our offenses.

Jesus of Nazareth during the last supper said, "This is my body given up for you. . . . This is the cup of my blood shed for you."

Jesus, faithful priest, who through his own blood, enters the eternal tabernacle; Jesus, the priest who, according to the Order of Melchisidech, leaves us his own sacrifice: do this! Jesus, Heart of Jesus!

2 Heart of Jesus in Gethsemane, "sorrowful, even unto death," who felt the terrible "burden." When he said, "All things are possible to you; remove this cup from me!" (Mark 14:36), yet at the same time he knew that it was the Father's will, and his only desire was to fulfill it, to drain the cup to the very bottom.

Heart of Jesus, bruised because of the eternal judgment: for God so loved the world that he gave his only begotten Son.

3 Many centuries earlier the prophet Isaiah said: "Surely he has borne our griefs and carried our sorrows; yet we esteemed him stricken, smitten by God, and afflicted" (53:4).

He was sacrificed for our sins; and yet did they not say on Golgotha: "If you are the Son of God, come down from that cross!" (Matthew 27:40)?

4 They spoke like that and yet the prophet knew. Isaiah said many centuries earlier: "He was wounded for our transgressions, he was bruised for our iniquities; . . . All we like sheep have gone astray; we have turned every one to his own way; and the Lord has laid on him the iniquity of us all. . . . He was cut off from the land of the living, stricken for the transgression of my people" (53:5-8).

5 Bruised for our offenses! Heart of Jesus, bruised by our offenses. . . .

The whole body of the Crucified freely embraces the suffering of his agony. Death slowly reaches his Heart.

Jesus says: "It is finished!"

"Father, into your hands I commend my spirit" (Luke 23:46).

How differently could the Scriptures have been fulfilled?

How differently could the words of the prophet be fulfilled, as he said: "the righteous one, my servant, [shall] make many to be accounted righteous; through him the Lord's will shall be fulfilled" (Isaiah 53:11).

The Father's will. Not my will, but yours.

6 We are united here in prayer with you, Mother of Christ, with you who shared in his sufferings. Lead us to the Heart of your Son in agony on the cross; there, in its despoliation, it is revealed as love.

You shared in his sufferings; permit us to persevere always in the embrace of this mystery.

Mother of the Redeemer!

Lead us to the Heart of your Son!

25

Heart of Jesus, obedient unto death

July 23, 1989

Heart of Jesus, obedient unto death, have mercy on us.

1 Dear brothers and sisters, this invocation of the Litany of the Sacred Heart invites us today to contemplate the Heart of the obedient Christ. The whole life of Jesus is characterized by perfect obedience to the will of the Father, the supreme and coeternal source of his being (John 1:1-2). Their power and glory and wisdom are one; their infinite love is mutual. Because of this communion of life and love, the Son adheres fully to the plan of the Father, who wills man's salvation through man. In the fullness of time he is born of the Virgin Mary (Galatians 4:4) with an obedient Heart to repair the damage caused to the human race by the disobedient hearts of their first parents.

Therefore, entering the world, Christ says: "Lo, I have come to do your will, O God" (Hebrews 10:7). "Obedience" is the new name of "love"!

2 The gospels show us that during his life Jesus was always intent on doing the Father's will. To Mary and Joseph, who for three days had been sorrowfully searching for him, the twelve-year-old Jesus replies: "How is it that you sought me? Did you not know that I must be in my Father's house?" (Luke 2:49). His whole life was dominated by that "I must," which determines his choices and guides his activity. One day he was to say to his disciples: "My food is to do the will of him who sent me, and to accomplish his work" (John 4:34); he was to teach them to pray thus: "Our Father . . . your will be done on earth as it is in heaven" (Matthew 6:10).

3 Jesus is obedient unto death (Philippians 2:8), although nothing is more radically opposed to him than death, since he is the very source of life (John 11:25-26).

In those tragic hours there come worrying dejection and anxiety (Matthew 26:37), fear and perturbation (Mark 14:33), the sweat of blood and the tears (Luke 22:44). Then on the cross pain lacerates his pierced body. The bitterness of rejection, betrayal, ingratitude fills his Heart. Yet the peace of obedience dominates over all. "Not my will, but thine, be done" (Luke 22:42). Jesus gathers his remaining strength and, as if summarizing his life, speaks his last words: "It is finished" (John 19:30).

4 At the beginning, middle, and end of Jesus' life one sole desire filled his Heart: to do the Father's will. As we contemplate this life, united by filial obedience to the Father, we understand the apostle Paul's words: "By one man's obedience many will be made righteous" (Romans 5:19), and the other mysterious and profound statement of the letter to the Hebrews: "Although he was a Son, he learned obedience through what he suffered; and being made perfect he became the source of eternal salvation to all who obey him" (5:8-9).

May holy Mary, the Virgin of the anxious and generous "fiat," help us also to learn this fundamental lesson.

26

Heart of Jesus, pierced with a lance

July 30, 1989

Heart of Jesus, pierced with a lance, have mercy on us.

1 Throughout the centuries, few pages of the gospel have attracted more attention from mystics, spiritual writers, and theologians than the passage from Saint John's Gospel which describes Christ's glorious death and the piercing of his side (19:23-37). The invocation of the Litany which I have just recalled is inspired by that passage.

In the pierced Heart we contemplate the filial obedience of Jesus to the Father, whose task he courageously fulfilled (John 19:30), and his fraternal love for man, whom he "loved to the end" (John 13:1), that is, to the ultimate sacrifice of himself. The pierced Heart is the sign of the totality of this love in the vertical and horizontal directions, like the two arms of the cross.

2 The pierced Heart is also the symbol of the new life given to man through the Spirit and the sacraments. No sooner had the soldier struck the blow with the lance, than from Christ's wounded side "there came out blood and water" (John 19:34). The blow of the lance established the fact of Christ's death. He is truly dead, as he was truly born, and as he would truly rise again in his own body (John 20:24-27). Against every ancient or modern temptation to Docetism, to giving in to the "appearance," the evangelist calls all back to the stark certainty of reality. Yet at the same time he intends to deepen the significance of the salvific event and to explain it through the symbol.

Therefore, he regards the episode of the piercing with the lance as profoundly significant. Just as from the rock struck by Moses a stream of water gushed forth in the desert (Numbers 20:8-11), so from Christ's side, pierced by the lance, there came forth a torrent of water to quench the thirst of the new People of God. This torrent is the gift of the Spirit (John 7:37-39), which nourishes the divine life in us.

3 Finally, from the pierced Heart of Christ the Church is born. Just as from the side of the sleeping Adam his wife Eve was taken, so — according to a patristic tradition going back to the first centuries — from the wounded side of the Savior as he slept in death on the cross, the Church, his Spouse, was taken. In fact, the Church is formed from the water and the blood — Baptism and the Eucharist — which flow from the pierced Heart. Therefore the conciliar Constitution on the Liturgy rightly states: "It was from the side of Christ as he slept the sleep of death upon the cross that there came forth the wondrous sacrament of the whole Church" (*Sacrosanctum Concilium*, No. 5).

4 The evangelist notes that beside the cross was Mary, the Mother of Jesus (John 19:25). She saw the wounded Heart from which there flowed blood and water, blood taken from her blood, and she understood that her Son's blood had been shed for our salvation. Then she understood fully the significance of the words which her Son had spoken a short time previously: "Woman, this is your son" (John 19:26); the Church which flowed from the wounded Heart had been entrusted to her motherly care.

Let us ask Mary to lead us to draw more and more abundantly from the streams of grace flowing from Christ's wounded Heart.

27

Heart of Jesus, source of all consolation

August 13, 1989

Heart of Jesus, source of all consolation, have mercy on us.

1 God, the Creator of heaven and earth, is also "the God of all consolation" (2 Corinthians 1:3; Romans 15:5). Numerous pages of the Old Testament show us God with great tenderness and compassion consoling his people in the time of affliction. In order to comfort Jerusalem when destroyed and desolate, the Lord sends his prophets to bring a message of consolation: "Comfort, comfort my people. Speak tenderly to Jerusalem, and cry to her that her slavery is ended" (Isaiah 40:1-2). Turning to Israel when weighed down by fear of its enemies, he declares: "I, I am he that comforts you" (Isaiah 51:12). Again, comparing himself to a mother full of tenderness for her children, he shows his desire to bring peace, joy, and comfort to Jerusalem: "Rejoice with Jerusalem, and be glad for her, all you who love her . . . that you may be satisfied with her consolations. As one whom his mother comforts, so I will comfort you: you shall be comforted in Jerusalem" (Isaiah 66:10, 11, 13).

2 In Jesus, true God and true Man, our Brother, the "God-who-consoles" became present in our midst. In fact, he was thus referred to by the just man Simeon, who had the joy of taking the infant Jesus in his arms and recognizing him as the fulfillment of "the consolation of Israel" (Luke 2:25). Throughout the whole life of Christ, his preaching of the

Kingdom was a ministry of consolation: announcing good news to the poor, proclaiming freedom for captives, healing for the sick, and grace and salvation for all (Luke 4:16-21; Isaiah 61:1-2).

From Christ's Heart there flowed this soothing beatitude: "Blessed are those who mourn, for they shall be comforted" (Matthew 5:4); and also the reassuring invitation: "Come to me, all who labor and are heavy laden, and I will give you rest" (Matthew 11:28).

The consolation which came from the Heart of Christ was a sharing in human suffering, a desire to lessen anxiety and alleviate sadness, a practical sign of friendship. In his consoling words and deeds he marvelously combined deep feeling and effective action. Near the gate of the city of Nain, when he sees a widow accompanying the remains of her only son to the tomb, Jesus shares her grief: "He had compassion on her" (Luke 7:13); he touched the bier, ordered the boy to get up, and restored him to his mother (Luke 7:14-15).

3 The Heart of the Savior is still, or rather the original, "source of consolation," because Christ, together with the Father, gives the Consoler Spirit: "l will pray to the Father, and he will give you another Consoler to be with you for ever" (John 14:16, 25; 16:12): the Spirit of truth and peace, of harmony and gentleness, of comfort and consolation: a Spirit flowing from Christ's Pasch (John 19:28-34) and from the event of Pentecost (Acts 2:13).

4 Therefore, Christ's whole life was a continual ministry of mercy and consolation. The Church, contemplating Christ's Heart and the streams of grace and consolation which flow from it, has expressed this stupendous truth by the invocation "Heart of Jesus, source of all consolation, have mercy on us."

• This invocation is a reminder of the fountain from which

the Church throughout the centuries has drawn consolation and hope in time of trial and persecution;

• It is an invitation to seek true, lasting, and effective consolation in the Heart of Christ;

• It is an admonition that we, having experienced consolation from the Lord, should in our turn bring it with conviction and love to others, making our own the spiritual experience which made the apostle Paul say: the Lord "comforts us in all our afflictions, so that we may be able to comfort those who are in any affliction, with the comfort with which we ourselves are comforted by God" (2 Corinthians 1:4).

Let us ask Mary, comforter of the afflicted, to lead us in dark moments of sorrow and anxiety to Jesus, her dear Son, "source of all consolation."

28

Heart of Jesus, our life and resurrection

August 27, 1989

Heart of Jesus, our life and resurrection, have mercy on us.

1 This invocation from the Litany of the Sacred Heart, strong and persuasive as an act of faith, contains the entire mystery of Christ the Redeemer in a terse phrase. It recalls the words Jesus addressed to Martha, crushed by the death of her brother Lazarus: "I am the resurrection and the life; whoever believes in me, even if he dies, shall live" (John 11:25).

Jesus is the life which springs eternally from the divine wellspring of the Father: "In the beginning was the Word, and the Word was with God, and the Word was God. . . . In him was life, and the life was the light of men" (John 1:1-4).

Jesus in himself is life: "For just as the Father has life in himself, so he has granted his Son also to have life in himself" (John 5:26), he declares. In the intimate being of Christ, in his Heart, divine life and human life are harmoniously joined in total and inseparable unity. However, Jesus is also life for us. The purpose of the mission which he, the Good Shepherd, has received from the Father is "to give his life": "I have come that they may have life, and have it abundantly" (John 10:10).

2 Jesus is also the resurrection. Nothing is so radically opposed to the holiness of Christ, the Holy One of the Lord (Luke 1:35; Mark 1:24), as sin: nothing is so opposed to him, source of life, as death.

There is a mysterious bond between sin and death

83

(Wisdom 2:24; Romans 5:12, 6:23; etc.); both are realities which are essentially contrary to God's plan for man, who was not made for death but rather for life. In the face of every expression of death, Christ's Heart was deeply moved, and for love of the Father and mankind, his brothers and sisters, he made his life a "combat stupendous" (*Roman Missal*, Easter Sequence) against death. With a single word he restored physical life to Lazarus, to the son of the widow of Nain, and to the daughter of Jairus; by the strength of his merciful love he gave spiritual life back to Zacchaeus, to Mary of Magdala, to the adulterous woman, and to all those who acknowledged his saving presence.

3 Brothers and sisters, no one experienced that the Heart of Jesus is "life and resurrection" as Mary did:

• From him, the life, Mary received the life of original grace and by listening to his word and attentively observing his salvific actions she was able to preserve and nourish it;

• From him, the resurrection, she was associated in a singular way to his victory over death. The mystery of her assumption — body and soul — into heaven is the consoling proof that Christ's victory over sin and death is extended in the members of his Mystical Body, first of all in Mary, the "most eminent member" of the Church (*Lumen Gentium*, No. 53).

Glorified in heaven, with her motherly heart the Virgin is at the service of the redemption effected by Christ. "Mother of life," she is close to every woman who brings a child into the world, and is near every baptismal font where Christ's members are born of water and the Spirit (John 3:5); "Health of the sick," she is present wherever life is languishing, stricken by suffering and illness; "Mother of mercy," she calls those who have fallen under the weight of guilt to return to the fountains of life; "Refuge of sinners," she shows those who have strayed from it the way that leads to Christ: "Sorrowful Virgin," near her dying

Son (John 19:25), she is to be found wherever life is drawing to a close. Let us invoke her now with the Church: "Holy Mary, Mother of God, pray for us sinners, now and at the hour of our death."

29

Heart of Jesus, our peace and reconciliation

September 3, 1989

Heart of Jesus, our peace and reconciliation, have mercy on us.

1 Dear brothers and sisters, in reciting this beautiful invocation of the Litany of the Sacred Heart with faith, a sense of confidence and security overwhelms our soul: Jesus is truly our peace, our supreme reconciliation.

Jesus is our peace. The biblical meaning of the word "peace" is well known; in synthesis it means the sum total of the goods which Jesus the Messiah has brought to humanity. For this reason the gift of peace signals the beginning of his mission on earth, accompanies its development, and constitutes its crowning glory. "Peace" sing the angels near the crib of the newborn "Prince of Peace" (Luke 2:14; Isaiah 9:5). "Peace" is the greeting that springs from the Heart of Christ, moved to pity by the pain of the person who is suffering physically (Luke 8:48) or spiritually (Luke 7:50). "Peace" is the shining greeting of the risen Lord to his disciples (Luke 24:36; John 20:19, 26), whom, at the hour in which he leaves this earth, he entrusts to the action of the Holy Spirit, fountain of "love, joy, and peace" (Galatians 5:22).

2 At the same time, Jesus is our reconciliation. As a result of sin a deep and mysterious break was produced between God the Creator and man his creature. The whole of salvation history is nothing else than the wonderful recounting of God's intervention on behalf of mankind so that the latter may freely and lovingly return to him; because of the condition of the break, a situation of reconciliation and friendship, of communion and peace, comes about.

In the Heart of Christ, filled with love for the Father and for people, his brothers and sisters, the perfect reconciliation of heaven and earth takes place; the apostle Paul says, "We have been reconciled with God through the death of his Son" (Romans 5:10).

Whoever wants to experience reconciliation and peace must accept the Lord's invitation and go to him (Matthew 11:28). In Christ's Heart that person will find peace and rest; there his doubt will be changed into certainty, desire into contentment, sadness into joy, disturbance into serenity. There he will find relief for his suffering, courage to overcome fear, generosity not to give in to discouragement and to continue on the path of hope.

3 The heart of Mary is like the Heart of her Son in all things. The Blessed Virgin is also a presence of peace and reconciliation for the Church; is it not Mary who, through the angel Gabriel, received the greatest message of reconciliation and peace which God ever sent to the human race (Luke 1:26-58)?

Mary gave birth to him who is our reconciliation; she stood near the cross when, in the blood of the Son, God reconciled "all things to himself" (Colossians 1:20); now glorified in heaven, as a liturgical prayer reminds us, he "has a heart full of mercy toward sinners who, turning their gaze to her motherly charity, take refuge in her and implore the pardon" of God (cf. *Roman Missal*, Preface of the Blessed Virgin Mary).

May Mary, Queen of Peace, obtain for us from Christ the messianic gift of peace and the grace of full and lasting reconciliation with God and with our brothers and sisters. For this let us pray.

30

Heart of Jesus, victim for sin

September 10, 1989

Heart of Jesus, victim for sin, have mercy on us.

1 Dear brothers and sisters, this invocation from the Litany of the Sacred Heart reminds us that Jesus, according to the words of Saint Paul, "was put to death for our sins" (Romans 4:25); indeed, even though he had not committed sin, "God made him to be sin on our behalf" (2 Corinthians 5:21). Upon the Heart of Christ the weight of the sin of the world weighed heavily.

In him was fulfilled perfectly the figure of the "paschal lamb," the victim offered to God so that in the sign of its blood the firstborn of the Hebrews might be saved (Exodus 12:21-27). Rightly, therefore, John the Baptist recognizes in him the true "Lamb of God" (John 1:29): the innocent lamb who took upon himself the sin of the world in order to immerse it in the saving waters of the Jordan (Matthew 3:13-16 and parallels); the meek lamb "led to the slaughter, like a sheep that is silent before its shearers" (Isaiah 53:7), so that the haughty word of evil men might be confounded by his divine silence.

Jesus is the willing victim because he offered himself "freely to his passion" (*Roman Missal*, Eucharistic Prayer II), the victim of expiation for the sins of mankind (Leviticus 1:5; Hebrews 10:5-10), which he purged in the fire of his love.

2 Jesus is the eternal victim. Risen from the dead and glorified at the right hand of the Father, he preserves in his immortal body the marks of the wounds of his nailed hands and feet, of his pierced side (John 20:27; Luke 24:39-40) and presents them to the Father in his incessant prayer of intercession on our behalf (Hebrews 7:25; Romans 8:34).

The wonderful Sequence of the Easter Mass, recalling this element of our faith, exhorts us: "Christians, to the Paschal Victim, offer your thankful praises. / A Lamb the sheep redeems: Christ, who alone is sinless, reconciles us sinners to the Father" (Sequence "Victimae Paschali," v. l).

The Preface of Easter proclaims that Christ is "the true Lamb who took away the sins of the world. By dying he destroyed our death; by rising he restored our life."

3 Brothers and sisters, at this time of the traditional Marian prayer we have contemplated the Heart of Jesus, victim for sin; however, his sorrowful Mother contemplated it first of all and most deeply of all. The liturgy sings of her: "For the sins of his own nation she saw Jesus hang in desolation" (Sequence "Stabat Mater," v. 7).

As the liturgical memorial of the sorrowful Blessed Virgin Mary draws near, let us recall her fearless and intercessory presence at the foot of the cross on Calvary, and gratefully reflect on that moment the dying Christ, victim for the sins of the world, gave her to us as a Mother: "Behold your Mother" (John 19:27).

To Mary let us entrust our prayer as we say to her Son, Jesus: Heart of Jesus, victim for sin, accept our praise, our everlasting thanks, our sincere repentance. Have mercy on us now and for ever. Amen.

31

Heart of Jesus, salvation of those who trust in you

September 17, 1989

Dear brothers and sisters:

1 At this time of the Angelus, let us pause a few moments to reflect on the invocation of the Litany of the Sacred Heart which says, "Heart of Jesus, salvation of those who trust in you, have mercy on us."

The Holy Scriptures repeatedly affirm that the Lord is "a God who saves" (Exodus 15:2; Psalms 51:16, 79:9; Isaiah 46:13) and that salvation is a gratuitous gift of his love and mercy. The apostle Paul, in a text of great doctrinal value, decisively affirms that God "wants all people to be saved and come to knowledge of the truth" (1 Timothy 2:4, 4:10).

This salvific will which is manifested in God's many wondrous interventions in history reached its perfection in Jesus of Nazareth, the incarnate Word, Son of God and Son of Mary. In him in fact the Lord's message to his "Servant" is perfectly fulfilled: "I shall make you a light to the nations, so that you may bring my salvation to the ends of the earth" (Isaiah 49:6; Luke 2:32).

2 Jesus is the epiphany of the Father's salvific love (Titus 2:11, 3:4). When Simeon took the Baby Jesus into his arms, he exclaimed: "My eyes have seen your salvation" (Luke 2:30).

In Jesus in fact everything pertains to his mission as Savior: the name that he bears (Jesus means "God saves"), the words he speaks, the actions he performs, the sacraments he institutes.

Jesus is fully conscious of the mission which the Father has entrusted to him: "The Son of man has come to seek and to save the lost" (Luke 19:10). From his Heart, that is, from the most intimate part of his being, arises that commitment to the salvation of man which impels him to climb Mount Calvary like a meek lamb, to extend his arms on the cross and to "give his life as a ransom for many" (Mark 10:45).

3 We can, therefore, place our hope in the Heart of Christ. That Heart, the invocation says, is salvation "for those who trust in him." The Lord himself the night before his passion asked the apostles to have trust in him: "Do not let your hearts be troubled. Have faith in God and have faith in me" (John 14:1). Today he asks us to trust him fully; he asks it because he loves us, because for our salvation his Heart was pierced and his hands and feet were nailed. Whoever trusts in Christ and believes in the power of his love renews in himself the experience of Mary of Magdala, whom the Easter liturgy portrays as saying, "Christ, my hope, is risen!" (Sequence of Easter Sunday).

Let us therefore take refuge in the Heart of Christ. He offers us a word which does not pass away (Matthew 24:25), a love which does not fail, a friendship which does not end, a presence which does not cease (Matthew 28:20).

May the Blessed Virgin, "who received in her immaculate heart the Word of God and merited to conceive him in her virginal womb" (Preface of the Votive Mass of the Blessed Virgin Mary, Mother of the Church), teach us to place all our hope in the Heart of her Son in the certainty that it will not be disappointed.

32

Heart of Jesus, hope of those who die in you

November 5, 1989

Dear brothers and sisters:

1 The recent Commemoration of All the Faithful Departed invites us today to look, in the light of faith and hope, at the death of the Christian, for which the Litany of the Sacred Heart, the object of our reflection on preceding Sundays, places on our lips the invocation "Heart of Jesus, hope of those who die in you, have mercy on us."

Death is part of the human condition: it is the final moment of the historical phase of life. In the Christian understanding, death is a passage from created light to uncreated light, from temporal life to eternal life.

Now, if the Heart of Christ is the source from which the Christian draws the light and energy to live as a child of God, to what other fountain should he turn to draw the strength to die in a manner that is consistent with his faith? As he "lives in Christ," he cannot but "die in Christ."

The invocation of the Litany sums up Christian experience in the presence of death: the Heart of Christ, his love and mercy, are the hope and security for whoever dies in him.

2 However, it is right to pause a moment and ask ourselves, what does it mean "to die in Christ"? First of all, it means, dear brothers and sisters, to interpret the appalling and mysterious event of death in the light of the teaching of the Son of God and see it therefore as the moment of departure for the Father's house, where Jesus, also passing through death, has gone to prepare a place for us (John 14:2). It means, that is, to believe that despite the decomposition of our body, death is the premise of life and abundant fruit (John 12:24).

Furthermore, "to die in Christ" means to trust in Christ and abandon oneself totally to him, placing in his hand — the hands of a brother, friend, good shepherd — one's destiny, just as he when dying committed his spirit into his Father's hands (Luke 23:46). It means to close one's eyes to the light of this world in peace, in friendship and communion with Jesus, because nothing, "neither life nor death . . . can ever separate us from the love of God in Christ Jesus our Lord" (Romans 8:38-39). In that supreme hour the Christian knows that even if his heart accuses him of guilt, the Heart of Christ is greater than his and can cancel his every debt, if he is repentant (1 John 3:20).

3 "To die in Christ" also means, dear brothers and sisters, to prepare oneself for that decisive moment with the "holy signs" of the "Easter passage": the Sacrament of Penance which reconciles us to the Father and with all creatures; Holy Viaticum, Bread of Life, and medicine of immortality; Anointing of the Sick which gives strength to body and spirit for the supreme battle.

"To die in Christ" means, finally, "to die like Christ" praying and pardoning, with the Blessed Virgin at one's side. As a mother, she was near the cross of her Son (John 19:25); as a mother, she is close to her children when they are dying, she who through the sacrifice of her heart cooperated in giving them birth to the life of grace (*Lumen Gentium*, No. 53); she is at their side with her motherly and compassionate presence, so that through the labor pains of death they may be born to the life of glory.

33

Heart of Jesus, delight of all the saints

November 12, 1989

Dear brothers and sisters:

1 Today the Church rejoices in the glorification of two of her children, Agnes of Bohemia and Albert Chmielowski. They go to join that "immense multitude" which the liturgy invited us to contemplate on the recent Solemnity of All Saints. Before such an exalting sight the invocation from the Litany spontaneously springs to our lips: "Heart of Jesus, delight of all the saints, have mercy on us."

From hope to fulfillment, from desire to realization, from earth to heaven: this seems to be the tempo at which the last three invocations of the Litany of the Sacred Heart come one after another, dear brothers and sisters. Following the invocations "salvation of those who trust in you" and "hope of those who die in you," the Litany ends addressing the Heart of Jesus as "delight of all the saints." It is already a vision of paradise, a quick glimpse of life in heaven, a brief word that opens up infinite spaces of eternal bliss.

2 The disciple of Jesus lives on this earth waiting to join his Master, yearning to contemplate his face, in the consuming desire to live for ever with him. But in heaven the expectation fulfilled, the disciple has already "entered into the joy of his Lord" (Matthew 25:21, 23); he contemplates the Master's face, no longer transfigured for only a moment (Matthew 17:2; Mark 9:2; Luke 9:28), but eternally resplendent with the brightness of eternal Light (Hebrews 1:2); the disciple lives with Jesus from Jesus' very own life.

Life in heaven is none other than the perfect, unending, intense enjoyment of the love of God — Father, Son, and Spirit; it is none other than the complete revelation of Christ's intimate being and the full communication with the life and love that spring from his Heart. In heaven the blessed see every desire fulfilled, every prophecy verified, all thirst for happiness satisfied, and every aspiration realized.

3 Therefore the Heart of Christ is the source of the life and love of the saints; in Christ and through him the blessed in heaven are loved by the Father, who unites them to himself with the bond of the Spirit, divine Love; in Christ and through him they love the Father and all people, their brothers and sisters, with the love of the Spirit.

The Heart of Christ is the life-giving space of the blessed, the place where they remain in love (John 15:9), deriving eternal and unlimited joy. The infinite thirst for love, the mysterious thirst which God has placed in the human heart, is satisfied in the divine Heart of Christ.

In that Heart is manifested the fullness of the love of the Redeemer for mankind in need of salvation; of the Master for his disciples, thirsting for truth; of the Friend who overcomes separation, raising his servants to the status of friends forever and in everything. The intense desire which is expressed on earth in the plea "Come, Lord Jesus" (Revelation 22:20) is now in heaven transformed into a face-to-face vision, into peaceful possession, into a fusion of life: of Christ in the blessed, of the blessed in Christ!

Raising the glance of our mind toward them and contemplating them gathered around Christ, together with their Queen, the Most Holy Virgin, let us repeat today with firm hope the joyful invocation "Heart of Jesus, delight of all the saints, have mercy on us."

Historical note

To help understand the Litany of the Sacred Heart of Jesus as a prayer-form we will first situate it in the history of litanies in the Church.

Litanies in the Church

The oldest *litanies* in the liturgical sense were forms of supplication or *processions* of clergy and people to beg God's mercy, to celebrate some particular divine mystery, or to honor the memory of the saints.

One of the clearest early examples we have is found in a series of processions instituted by Pope Saint Gregory the Great during the pestilence of Rome in 590. Seven different processions — which were called litanies, and divided according to the different classes of persons participating in each (clergy, laymen, monks, consecrated virgins, married women, widows, and the poor) — each departed from a different Church in Rome and all converged on the Basilica of Saint Mary Major.

Prayers were recited or sung by the people as the processions moved along. Thus the transition was easily made from this original sense of procession to what we more usually understand by litanies.

The word *litany* has a general meaning of prayer but refers specifically to a prayer of supplication or intercession. As a prayer-form it is usually a brief formula which the Christian assembly repeats as a response to a series of intentions enunciated by a sacred minister or leader of prayer. Among the earliest forms of this "prayer of the faithful" (as it was also called) was *Lord, have mercy* (the *Kyrie eleison* in Greek or *Domine, miserere* in Latin). A "prayer of the faithful" was also used in the Eucharistic liturgy and has been restored to its place after the homily in the revised Eucharistic celebration after Vatican II. But throughout the centuries the Latin liturgy retained this ancient prayer form in the Solemn Orations of Good Friday.

The Major Litanies, as they were called, originated in Rome as a festive procession on April 25, moving along the streets from the Church of Saint Lawrence in Lucina to the Basilica of Saint Peter. Up to the time of Vatican II the Litany of the Saints was retained in the liturgy on this day, from the time it was chanted in procession on the Feast of Saint Mark. The festive nature of the procession was later changed to penitential, like the so-called Minor Litanies observed as times of special prayer on three days before Ascension Thursday, intended originally to ask God's mercy in averting earthquakes and other natural disasters.

Today what we usually understand by a *litany* would be the Litany of the Saints, the Litany of the Blessed Virgin (known also as the Litany of Loreto), or the Litany of the Sacred Heart. Common to all of them is a series of invocations usually recited by one person, to which others respond, for example, with "pray for us" in the case of invocations of the saints or "have mercy on us" when the invocations are directed to God.

In English we use the word *litany* in the singular to refer to the entire collection of invocations, whereas in some languages such as Italian, Spanish, and French, it is customary to apply it to each invocation and to refer to the entire collection of invocations in the plural as *litanies.*

The Litany of the Saints is still chanted or recited today in the Easter Vigil liturgy of Holy Saturday during the blessing of the baptismal font, during the rites for the ordination of deacons, priests, and bishops, and in the prayers for the dying. The most popular litany is the Litany of Loreto (of the Blessed Virgin Mary), which took various forms until stabilized and officially approved by Pope Sixtus V in 1587.

Eventually litanies as a popular form of prayer had so proliferated that Pope Clement VIII on September 6, 1601, intervened with a decree of pastoral concern that distinguished between the numerous litanies which could continue to be used privately and litanies officially approved by the Church for public worship and found in the Breviary or Roman Ritual.

When, at the end of the last century, the Litany of the Heart of Jesus was officially approved, there were only three other litanies approved for public worship: Litany of the Saints, Litany of Loreto, and Litany of the Holy Name of Jesus. Today the distinction is no longer made between public and private recitation, but the latest edition of the *Enchiridion Indulgentiarum* lists six litanies which had previously been approved for public recitation and which continue to carry an indulgence: Holy Name of Jesus, Sacred Heart of Jesus, Precious Blood of Our Lord Jesus Christ (introduced by Pope John XXIII), Blessed Virgin Mary, Saint Joseph, and the Saints.

Litany of the Sacred Heart

It would take too long even to list the different private forms of litanies in honor of the Heart of Jesus, some of them antedating Saint Margaret Mary Alacoque. We will restrict ourselves to mentioning those litanies which in some way stem from the influence of Saint Margaret Mary and which more directly influenced the formation of the present Litany.

The origins of the Litany of the Heart of Jesus as we know it date back to the time of Saint Margaret Mary Alacoque. As far as we can ascertain from her extant writings she did not compose a litany herself but was familiar with a series of invocations honoring the Heart of Jesus composed by Sister Joly of the Visitation Monastery at Dijon and another composed by Mother de Soudeilles, superior of the Visitation Monastery at Moulins. There was a third list of twenty-three invocations composed by Father Jean Croiset, spiritual director of Saint Margaret Mary after Blessed Claude La Colombiere, and published in the second edition of his book on Devotion to the Heart of Jesus. With ten invocations added later, this third Litany — like the other two — had thirty-three invocations in honor of the thirty-three years of the earthly life of our Lord.

A person who gave great impetus to praying these litanies was the Servant of God Anna Maddalena de Remuzat of the Visitation Monastery at Marseilles. She had published a formula for a Litany of the Heart of Jesus, which consisted of twenty-seven invocations culled from the litanies just mentioned. It came to be known as the Litany of Marseilles.

During the plague that broke out in Marseilles and ravaged the city (1720), the bishop ordered public prayers in honor of the Sacred Heart, including the Litany popularized by Anna Maddalena de Remuzat. The bishop consecrated the city and the diocese to the Heart of Jesus, and when the plague suddenly and noticeably diminished and then ended completely, the bishop declared that deliverance from the plague was due to a miracle of the Heart of Jesus.

For years after the plague ceased, the people of Marseilles continued to pray this Litany but, according to the existing norms of the Church at that time, only in private. Marseilles became known as the City of the Sacred Heart.

To bring the private devotion of the people in harmony with liturgical norms, another bishop of Marseilles later petitioned (in 1898) the Holy See to give official approval to the Litany in use in Marseilles. A similar request, but with another form of the Litany, was made by the bishop of Autun, the diocese in which Paray-le-Monial is located. The

Congregation of Rites was favorable to the requests and compared the two forms. Basically the first was the one accepted, with modifications and additions, so that the Litany would have thirty-three invocations. In this modified form the Litany was approved by Pope Leo XIII on June 27, 1898, for the dioceses of Marseilles and Autun and for the Visitation Order.

Less than a year later, in response to numerous requests received from other places, Leo XIII on April 2, 1899, approved the Litany for the universal Church. It is this officially approved version of the Litany of the Heart of Jesus that Pope John Paul II commented on in Angelus messages from 1985 to 1989.

Structure and content of the Litany

The Litany of the Heart of Jesus follows the overall structure of litanies: in the beginning, first the threefold invocation: *Lord, have mercy; Christ, have mercy; Lord, have mercy;* then invocation of the divine persons. A litany concludes with a threefold *Lamb of God*, then a verse and response, and a final prayer which is sometimes varied. The body of the Litany of the Heart of Jesus consists of thirty-three invocations with the response to each: *have mercy on us*.

Various attempts have been made to discern a pattern in the arrangement of the thirty-three invocations of the Litany. Considering the origins of the Litany from various sources, it would be difficult to say what the original plan was. But very briefly, without excluding other possible explanations, we may see the following divisions in the present order of the invocations.

The Litany may be divided into two major parts with further subdivisions. In the first part (1-16), the invocations begin with the trinitarian aspects of the Heart of Jesus as related to God the Father and to the Holy Spirit (1-2), followed by references to the divine Person of the Word (3-7), and to the treasures of his Heart considered in itself (8-15). The last invocation (16) of this first part expressed the Father's delight in his Son in words the Gospels repeat at the baptism end transfiguration of Jesus.

The second part of the Litany (17-33) looks at the treasures of the Heart of Jesus as turned toward us (17-21) and as source of pardon, salvation, and all goodness (22-32). Everything the Heart of Jesus is can be summed up in the concluding invocation: delight of all the saints.

Letter of John Paul II on the Sacred Heart on the occasion of the third centenary of the death of Saint Margaret Mary

To Bishop Raymond Seguy
BISHOP OF AUTUN, CHALON, AND MACON

The third centenary of the death of Saint Margaret Mary, canonized by my predecessor Benedict XV in 1920, recalls the memory of one who, from 1673 to 1675, was favored with appearances of the Lord Jesus and was entrusted with a message whose widespread influence in the Church has been tremendous. It was during the Octave of Corpus Christi in 1675, in that Grand Century when so many writers and artists penetrated the riches of the human soul, that the young Visitandine of Paray-le-Monial heard these bewildering words: "Behold this heart which has so loved human beings and which has spared itself nothing even to exhausting and spending itself to give witness to this love; and in recompense for the most part I have received only ingratitude."

When I was on pilgrimage in 1986 to the tomb of Margaret Mary, I asked, in the spirit of what has been handed down in the Church, that veneration of the Sacred Heart be faithfully restored. For it is in the Heart of Christ that the human heart learns to know the true and unique meaning of its life and destiny; it is in the Heart of Christ that the human heart receives its capacity to love.

Saint Margaret Mary learned the grace of loving by means of the cross. In it she delivers to us a message that is ever relevant. It is necessary, she says, "to make ourselves living copies of our crucified Spouse, by expressing him in ourselves in all our actions" (Letter of January 5, 1689).

She invites us to contemplate the Heart of Christ, that is, to recognize in the humanity of the Word incarnate, the infinite riches of his love for the Father and for all human beings. It is the love of Christ which makes a person worthy of being loved. Created in the image and likeness of God, the human person has received a heart eager for love and capable of loving. The love of the Redeemer, which heals it from the wound of sin, elevates it to its filial condition. With Saint Margaret Mary, united to the Savior also in his suffering offered for love, we shall ask for the grace of knowing the infinite value of every person.

To give to veneration of the Sacred Heart the place due to it in the Church, it is necessary to take up again the exhortation of Saint Paul: "Have within you the sentiments which were in Christ Jesus" (Philippians 2:5). All the gospel accounts should be reread from this perspective: each verse, meditated with love, will reveal an aspect of the mystery hidden for centuries and now revealed to our eyes (Colossians 1:26). The only Son of God, in becoming incarnate, takes a human Heart. Through the years he passed in the midst of men, "gentle and humble of heart" (Matthew 11:29), he revealed the riches of his interior life by each of his gestures, his looks, his words, his silences. In Christ Jesus is fulfilled the fullness of the commandment of the Old Testament: "You shall love the Lord with all your heart" (Deuteronomy 6:5). In fact, only the Heart of Christ has loved the Father with an undivided love.

And behold we are called to share in this love and to receive through the Holy Spirit this extraordinary capacity to love. After their encounter with the Risen One on the road to

Emmaus, the disciples were filled with amazement: "Were not our hearts burning inside us as he talked to us on the road and explained the Scriptures to us?" (Luke 24:32). Yes, the human heart is inflamed by contact with the Heart of Christ, for it discovers in this love for the Father that the risen Lord has accomplished "all that the prophets have announced" (Luke 24:25).

The humanity of the Lord Jesus dead and risen reveals itself to us through contemplation of his Heart. Nourished by meditation on the Word of God, prayer of adoration places us in the closest, most intimate relationship with this "Heart that has so loved human beings." Understood in this way, devotion to the Sacred Heart fosters active participation of the faithful at times of grace in the Eucharist and the Sacrament of Penance; intimately bound to the humanity of Christ given for the salvation of the world, the faithful thus derive the desire to be united to all those who suffer and the courage to be witnesses of the Good News.

I encourage pastors, religious communities, and all animators of pilgrimages to Paray-le-Monial to contribute to the diffusion of the message received by Saint Margaret Mary. And to you, pastor of the Church of Autun, and to all who will allow themselves to be moved by this teaching, I hope you will discover in the Heart of Christ the force of love, the sources of grace, the real presence of the Lord in his Church by the gift daily renewed of his Body and Blood. To each of you, I willingly grant my apostolic blessing.

Pope John Paul II
Feast of the Sacred Heart
June 22, 1990
The Vatican